Kento
Starcross

of Yesteryear

(From The Turf to The Sod)

Eric Vaughan

OBELISK PUBLICATIONS

Also in this Series

Ashburton of Yesteryear, *John Germon and Pete Webb*
Teign Valley of Yesteryear, Parts I and II, *Chips Barber*
Pinhoe of Yesteryear, Parts I and II, *Chips Barber*
Brixham of Yesteryear, Parts I, II and II, *Chips Barber*
Princetown of Yesteryear, Parts I and II, *Chips Barber*
Kingsteignton of Yesteryear, *Richard Harris*
Heavitree of Yesteryear, *Chips Barber*

Also about this Area

Around & About the Haldon Hills – Revisited, *Chips Barber*
An Alphington Album, *Pauline Aplin and Jeanne Gaskell*
Dawlish and Dawlish Warren, *Chips Barber*
Around & About Teignmouth and Shaldon, *Chips Barber*
Chudleigh Collection, *Chips Barber*
Topsham Past and Present, *Chips Barber*
Pub Walks in and around the Haldon Hills, *Brian Carter*

We have over 150 Devon titles. For a full list of current books, please contact us at
Obelisk Publications, 2 Church Hill, Pinhoe, Exeter, Devon, EX4 9ER or telephone (01392) 468556.

Acknowledgements

I wish to thank several friends for their help in the preparation of this book, firstly John Westcott, who is a mine of local information, Mr Ron White and the late Mrs White, Mrs Bosworth whose family kept the Devon Arms in Kenton and Mrs Ada Walters. Finally, my thanks also to my Father, who was born in Starcross and has many memories of the village and of the hospital which was for so long the hub of life in the area. Any other friends who have been omitted will, I hope, accept my apologies.

First published in 1998 by
Obelisk Publications, 2 Church Hill, Pinhoe, Exeter, Devon
Designed by Chips and Sally Barber
Typeset by Sally Barber
Printed in Great Britain by
The Devonshire Press Ltd, Torquay, Devon

© Chips Barber/Obelisk Publications

All Rights Reserved. No part of this publication may be reproduced, stored in a retrieval system, or transmitted, in any form or by any means, electronic, mechanical, photocopying, recording or otherwise, without the prior permission of the publishers and copyright holders.

Kenton & Starcross
of Yesteryear

This book, as the title suggests, takes us on a nostalgic, pictorial journey between the Turf Hotel and The Sod at Cockwood, featuring places and faces of yesteryear along the way. For those of you who don't know, 'The Sod' is a name for the harbour at Cockwood, which has been in use since at least 1803. I hope the pictures will help to revive memories for those people with an attachment to this lovely part of Devon and that you will excuse the occasional personal recollection, because this 'patch' is where I have my roots. Although I now live on the other side of the country, in Norfolk, I still have a very soft spot for the area covered in this book.

We start with these old picture postcard views of Turf, taken about 1900 in a more elegant age of dress! It was a popular promenade to stroll along the canal banks, or travel by boat to the Turf on fine evenings, Fridays and Saturdays being the busiest occasions.

Above is a view of the Avenue leading down to Powderham Church as it looked in about 1913. Those who travel this way now will know that the trees have grown considerably since then and the road has been widened. The picture below shows those pretty thatched cottages at the 'landward end' of this impressive straight. Below is the Belvedere in Powderham Park taken at a time when it was fully intact. This landmark sits on top of a ridge running along the side of the valley of the River Kenn. Belvedere derives from an Italian word which means 'fine view'. Certainly from this vantage point there is a terrific outlook.

The top picture was taken by the cottages at Powderham Sawmills and shows Rose Hellings standing with a young man whose legs are dangled over the parapet of the bridge. The middle and bottom picture are both taken at East Town, Kenton, and were both, like so many of the views in this book, published by the famous postcard publishers Chapman & Son, of Dawlish.

The top picture shows a distant view of the village as it looked in 1916. The middle photo shows the Village Stores early in the twentieth century. The pub beside it was called the Grooms Inn but before the Great War it was changed to the Dolphin. In the bottom picture it is just possible to spot the wheel of a cart protruding from Kenton Forge. The last blacksmith to work here was Charlie Hawkins who continued to ply his trade until this business ceased operating in 1935.

Kenton & Starcross of Yesteryear

Above is the smiling face of a young man who delivered fresh bread around the village many years ago. He was 'Baker Bidgood' who worked for Heale of Kenton. Heale's baker's shop was on the Triangle next to the haberdashery shop on the corner, run for many years by Miss Lamacraft. She is the girl with the dog in the picture on page 5.

Below the balloons and flags are out on the occasion of 'Kenton Fair'.

On this page are three pictures of the beautiful church of All Saints. Opposite, the pictures go back to an age when the motor car was non-existent, which made taking excellent photos like these, in and around Church Street, much easier. The corner shop in the top picture was a butcher's which closed many years ago. In the bottom picture the shop on the left was, for years, a harness maker, hence the modern name of Saddler's Cottage.

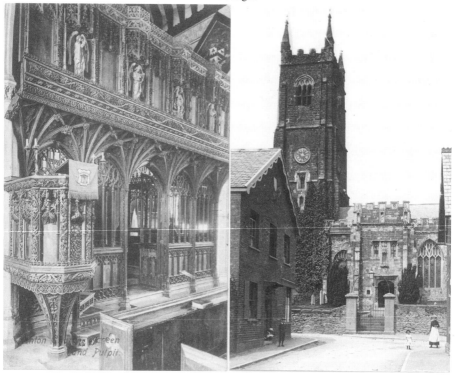

For those youngsters who loved a rural life, growing up in Kenton must have been a joy. However, at school it's likely that discipline was tough. Here are two groups of schoolchildren, many of whom came from outlying farms and cottages and who often trudged to school along muddy lanes.

Above, a procession can be seen making its way to the village green in Kenton. It was headed by Mr Toogood and the ceremony which followed was the unveiling of the War Memorial, seen in both the lower two pictures.

The house on the right, in the picture below, was the post office but was demolished in order to widen the road.

All aboard! Above, a party of Kentonians pose for the obligatory picture before setting off for a day out on one of the latest forms of transport of their day, an open-top bus from Blackboy Road, Exeter.

What a wonderful wedding day it must have been for Captain E. Newcombe and his new bride, Miss N. Courtenay! These pictures, below and opposite, convey some of the atmosphere of this special occasion, which took place on 14 September 1909. The make of the wonderful car, carrying the bride and bridegroom, is not known. The pictures of the Devon Arms Inn, taken from opposite directions, show us that the banner across the street wished the newly-wedded couple 'Good Luck' and 'God Bless the Happy Pair'.

WEDDING OF CAPTAIN E NEWCOMBE & MISS N COURTENAY
SEPT 14 1909 H

Above are members of the Kenton Band, complete with instruments, as they looked in 1911. The middle view is taken in South Town, Kenton. On the right Mrs Wallace and Nellie Wallace are standing, like everybody else, posed for the photographer. The farm on the left was owned by a family called Leach. It would be somewhat unwise to trundle a wheel-barrow down the centre of this road today! The bottom picture is looking up the brook towards the Triangle, with the Devon Arms hidden behind the hedge on the left.

This area is one of castles and fine houses. Here is Powderham Castle, long established home of the Earls of Devon. Above is a bridge over the River Kenn in the grounds of this fine stately home. Below are two pictures from Oxton, which lies less than two miles to the west of Kenton. The bottom picture shows, in all their finery, those who performed in the Oxton Pageant of 1909.

Mamhead House, high in the hills, is another of those grand houses and was the family home of the Newman family at one time, but times change and it has been a school, as has Oxton, and is now offices. Its grounds are beautiful and include the church of St Thomas the Apostle shown at the bottom of the page. Mamhead Rectory, shown here, followed the pattern in providing spacious accommodation for incumbents.

Although there are several rare pictures in this book there are none more 'precious' than the two on this page and the next two overleaf. And it's something of a minor miracle that they exist, because they were retrieved from a rubbish bin! These wonderful pictures show the long-gone light railway which was built between Black Forest, below Mamhead, and Starcross. It was built, during the First World War, to carry the timber felled in this forest; it was conveyed eastwards and down the valley of the Staplake Brook to join the main line. In the picture above Ern Holcombe is the engine driver, Nick Hawkins the fireman, George Holcombe is on the wagon, Jack Phillips is the horseman, who worked for Farmer Wright at Staplake Farm, a German POW is in the truck, Joe Holcombe, a trapper, is standing on the line and the overseer is Mr Chaffe.

(Overleaf) The forest enterprise was manned by the Canadian Lumber Corps who 'employed' German prisoners-of-war to do the felling and removing of timber, a much healthier option than trench warfare. The timber was brought down to the light railway on a horse-drawn inclined-plane railway. The troops and their charges were housed in timber huts. The Canadian troops attended dances at Starcross and Kenton and, because they consumed such large amounts of drink, were not charged admission. Following the cessation of hostilities, the lines were lifted.

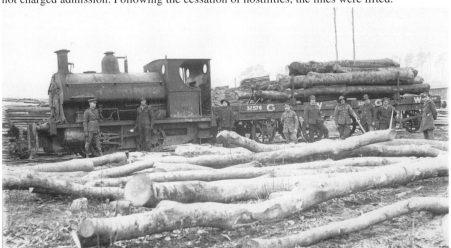

The three pictures on this page show Starcross as seen from a distance. The top two pictures are both from Warboro Hill whilst the one at the bottom is taken from Easter Hill. They all show a Starcross which was then a long, thin settlement but the extensive building of houses, in recent decades, means that the settlement has expanded a little around its midriff! The top picture gazes towards the mouth of the Exe Estuary and the tip of Dawlish Warren can just be spied in the top right corner. The second one shows the Western Counties Hospital on the far right. The bottom picture was taken on the lower slopes of Easter Hill. The towers of Starcross Church and Brunel's 'Atmospheric Pumping Station' are centre and right of this rural-looking scene from the past.

    'Staplake Mount' was probably best known as a 'Ministry of Agriculture, Fisheries and Food' establishment but these top two pictures predate their presence. Before the Second World War the house's electricity came from a most unusual source – the engine of a former E-boat! It was taken over during the war and a series of huts was built in front of the house to be used as a rest centre for fatigued firemen. The huts became laboratories where 'agricultural experiments' were conducted. The house was demolished in the 1970s.

    Not to be confused with the above, 'Staplake' became the female nurses' home for the Royal Western Counties Hospital. There was a willow bed beside the house which was used to supply the basket workshop at the hospital, Bill Willis and Jess Hurford being the last two exponents of this skill. Frank Towill was the brushmaker, Lou Luscombe the tailor and Nelson Mitchell the tinsmith, so the hospital was virtually self-sufficient. Even the mattresses were 'home-made' and the material for the staff uniforms was also made on the premises. Bill Veale, the cobbler, had a small shed at the bottom of No. 1 Coronation Street where he repaired shoes for the families of staff as a sideline.

Exeleigh stands on the Kenton side of Starcross behind limestone walls. However, in this pre-1910 photo it can be clearly seen and is also just visible on the right side of the middle picture. Close by was a cottage called 'Northend', once a police station complete with cell and barred windows. The man who owned it, Tom Drew, developed the ground opposite and discovered the foundations of a cottage.

The bottom picture shows two large buildings in the same vicinity. The house on the right was named as 'Soho House' on the 1890 Ordnance Survey map. It was owned in the 1940s and '50s by Miss Barbara Parker, who was a local benefactor. She had, in her front room, some wonderful model railway engines, each about four feet in length. These were built by her father, who was formerly an engineer in Birmingham. The house name was changed to Langdale in the early part of the twentieth century.

The six pictures spanning these two pages take us along the road into the centre of the village and it would be an interesting exercise to take this book along the same route to see the similarities and differences between then and now in each of the pictures.

Here we have two similar views but looking in opposite directions. The building in the centre of the above picture is the former Alexandra Hotel. To the right of it are a pair of double doors where, after the Second World War, Ernie Coombes ran a garage. Villagers also visited these premises to get their accumulators charged so that they could listen to their radios or wirelesses. The row of cottages behind the horse were destroyed in the fire of 1906, probably started by a spark from a passing railway engine. Below, the name of J & W Parkhouse can be seen on the side of the former pumping station. William Parkhouse, the coal merchant, worked to the grand old age of 90, when he retired to Dawlish, in 1936.

(Opposite) The top and bottom pictures show the Royal Western Counties Hospital, which opened on 1 June 1864 as the 'Western Counties Idiot Asylum'. Its working life spanned more than a century but it closed in 1986 and was demolished. The attractive cottage shown here was fire-damaged in 1936 and pulled down to make way for an office block for the hospital.

Two out of three of these pictures show the chimney from the hospital's busy steam laundry in the background. The middle picture, from the mid-1950s, includes Jack Gooding, Len Vaughan, Ray Davey, Frank Drew, Charlie Jarvoice, Maurice Wills, Roly Bidgood and Ted Sant.

The picture below, from about 1958, includes 'Jock' the coach driver, with the club mascot. Also shown are Bob Stephens, Paul Fairchild, Sam Willey, Eric Vaughan, Maurice Willey, Peter Martin, Ray Hill, Bert Napper, Geoff Palfrey, Don Burrows, David Symes and Alan Ley.

The children of Starcross know how to have a good time! Here we have three pictures featuring many well-known villagers. In the top picture the youngsters have dressed up for Starcross Carnival, about 1946 or 1947. Among them were Maureen Taylor, Jean Luscombe, Kathy Drew, Barbara Brooks, Douglas Jordan, David Holland, Eric Vaughan, Margaret Hamilton, Hazel Brooks, Margaret McLaughlin and Colin Price. The next two pictures are of Starcross School.

The children dressed in night attire, featured in the bottom picture, of about 1946, are Valerie Hockeridge, Doreen Randall, Ann Gilpin, Roy Brooks, Tony Tarr, Colin Price, Donald Northcott, Douglas Jordan, Eric Vaughan, Maureen Taylor, Joan Wall, June Davis, Arthur Lambshead, Raymond Locke, Michael Lott, Arthur Cowell, Betty Taylor and John Hart.

The top picture shows a coach outing and, judging by the smiling faces, a good time was being had by all. This Euchre party, from the Courtenay Arms, included Alan and Charlie Diaper, Mrs Hart, Harold Brooks, Ted Cowell, Arthur Osborne, Henry Lock, Phil Copp, Mr Wheaton, Bert Guest, Gerald Leach, Win Osborne, Kath Taylor, Harry Spear, Mrs Cann, Mrs Selby and Mrs Colley. The picture in the middle is of the wedding of Alan Ashford and Margot Mummery, which took place about 1956. Included in the back row are Eric Vaughan, Tony Burgess, Richard Finch, Len Vaughan, Rev Syme, Wilf Rogers (choirmaster), Rev Priddle, Bert Guest and John Moore.

In the front row are also Bruce Horrell, David White and Brian Richardson.

The bottom picture is another rare one and shows 'Starcross Market' in full swing. It was held in the small triangular field next to the school. The cattle were weighed on a weighbridge next to the Courtenay Arms Hotel and walked through the village to the market field. It stopped at the beginning of the Second World War but was later revived for a few years before it finally ceased.

The top two pictures are very similar but differ in that the top one has a row of three cottages, immediately above the ferry, which were burned down in 1906. In the lower picture there is a gap where they were once located. The lower pair of pictures reveal some of the maritime importance of Starcross. The unusual 'Swan of the Exe', built for Captain Peacock of Starcross, in 1860, by Dixon's of Exmouth, floats gracefully on the waters of the estuary. The bottom picture shows the Exmouth to Starcross ferry of yesteryear.

We cannot leave Starcross without briefly featuring the railway, which is such an obvious part of this waterside village. In the top picture 'Warwick Castle' is seen thundering through on its way towards the coast. Below is Starcross Station as it looked in 1958. The van outside the station was a familiar sight as it was the Ministry of Agriculture's vehicle to collect or despatch 'parcels' from here. The regular driver was Jack Graham of Cockwood.

Cofton and Cockwood, like Cockington in Torbay, derive their names from 'coc' meaning red and the countryside round about is certainly that. Below we have a view of the lovely Cofton Church of St Mary's, built on a raised bluff above former swampland, where I was christened. A 1933 guide to the area mentioned one of its treasures: "This little church possesses a remarkable chalice, made of mother-of-pearl, said to to have been taken from a Spanish ship; it is still used on special occasions."

Today 'Cofton Country', close to the church, is taken up by a camping and caravan park and many who stay here avail themselves of fishing in lakes formed by the damming of the 'red brook'.

The top picture opposite is 'Southbrook', which also appears on the left side of the picture below it, rising high above the northern side of Cockwood Harbour (The Sod). Today it's less visible because trees have

grown up close by which partly obscure it from view. Mrs Hoyle once lived here, from 1925, and was a generous local benefactor. She was a familiar sight in the district, usually seen driving around in her lovely Sunbeam Talbot convertible. The house, which became somewhat dilapidated, has been renovated in recent years by its present owners, Mr and Mrs Jeffrey.

The picture above shows Cockwood Harbour, believed to be the only one in England inside of a railway line! Cockwood village is full of character cottages and this picture shows just some of them.

There are ways of telling that these two pictures were taken at different times. The top picture is the older of the two as it shows that Shinton's Anchor Inn ('Teas Provided & Accommodation for Cyclists') is supplied by the Dawlish Brewery. The picture below reveals an enlarged building, its roof extended closer to the village hall.

This harbour, at high water, has been used for occasional total immersion baptisms.

We have reached 'The Sod' and thus the end of our pictorial journey. I hope you have wallowed in the nostalgia and enjoyed this sequence of old pictures.